Oceans

by Adele D. Richardson

Consultant:
Francesca Pozzi, Research Associate
Center for International Earth Science Information Network
Columbia University

Bridgestone Books
an imprint of Capstone Press
Mankato, Minnesota

Bridgestone Books are published by Capstone Press
151 Good Counsel Drive, P.O. Box 669, Mankato, Minnesota 56002
http://www.capstone-press.com

Library of Congress Cataloging-in-Publication Data
Richardson, Adele, 1966–
    Oceans/by Adele D. Richardson.
    p. cm.—(The Bridgestone science library)
    Includes bibliographical references and index.
    ISBN 0-7368-0838-8
    1. Ocean--Juvenile literature. [1. Ocean.] I. Title. II. Series.
GC21.5 .R52 2001
551.46—dc21   00-009806

Summary: Discusses the plants, animals, and climate of a rain forest ecosystem.

Editorial Credits
Karen L. Daas, editor; Karen Risch, product planning editor; Linda Clavel, designer and
    illustrator; Heidi Schoof, photo researcher

Photo Credits
Index Stock Imagery, 12
James P. Rowan, 6, 16
Linda Clavel, 1
PhotoDisc Inc., 5, 7, 9, 11, 13, 15, 17, 19, 21
Photo Network/Scott Winer, cover; Hal Beral, 14; Chad Ehlers, 18
Visuals Unlimited/David B. Fleetham, 10; Patrick Endres, 20

1 2 3 4 5 6 06 05 04 03 02 01

Table of Contents

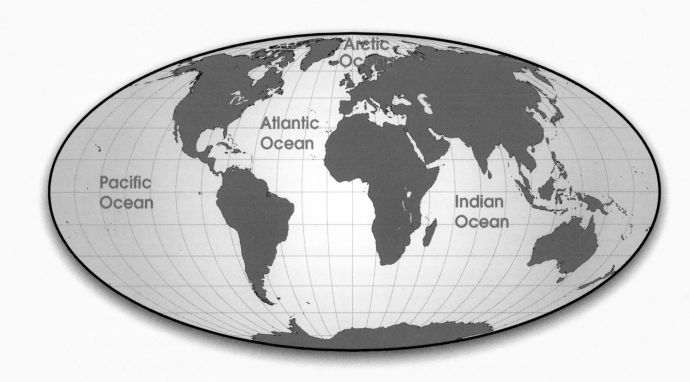

Arctic
Ocean

Atlantic
Ocean

Pacific
Ocean

Indian
Ocean

■ oceans

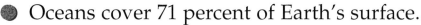

- Oceans cover 71 percent of Earth's surface.
- Each year, fishers catch about 200 billion pounds (90 billion kilograms) of seafood in oceans.
- Oceans hold 97 percent of Earth's water.
- The largest ocean is the Pacific Ocean. It contains nearly half of all the world's ocean water.
- The ocean's surface temperature is about 28 degrees Fahrenheit (-2 degrees Celsius) at the poles all year. Oceans in the rest of the world change temperature. The water is colder during winter than it is during summer.
- About 25 percent of all the world's oil comes from beneath the ocean floor.
- Ocean water has tiny specks of gold floating in it.
- About 3.5 pounds (1.6 kilograms) of salt are in every 100 pounds (45 kilograms) of seawater.

One large body of water covers Earth. This body is broken into oceans named Pacific, Atlantic, Indian, and Arctic. Some scientists also add the Antarctic Ocean at the South Pole to this list. Other scientists believe this area is the southern part of the Pacific and Atlantic Oceans. Together, all of these oceans make up the World Ocean.

Plants and animals live in oceans. Seaweed grows in shallow ocean waters. Animals such as fish, shrimp, and whales also live in the ocean.

Ocean water is always moving. Waves show the movement of water in the ocean. Waves do not move back and forth. They move up and down. The up and down movement forms a circle.

Waves begin at sea. Water near the surface moves in circles. The circles move nearby water. Near the shore, the ocean floor rises. The water at the bottom drags along the ocean floor. The water on top keeps moving and crashes on shore.

Waves crash on shore when water cannot complete its circle.

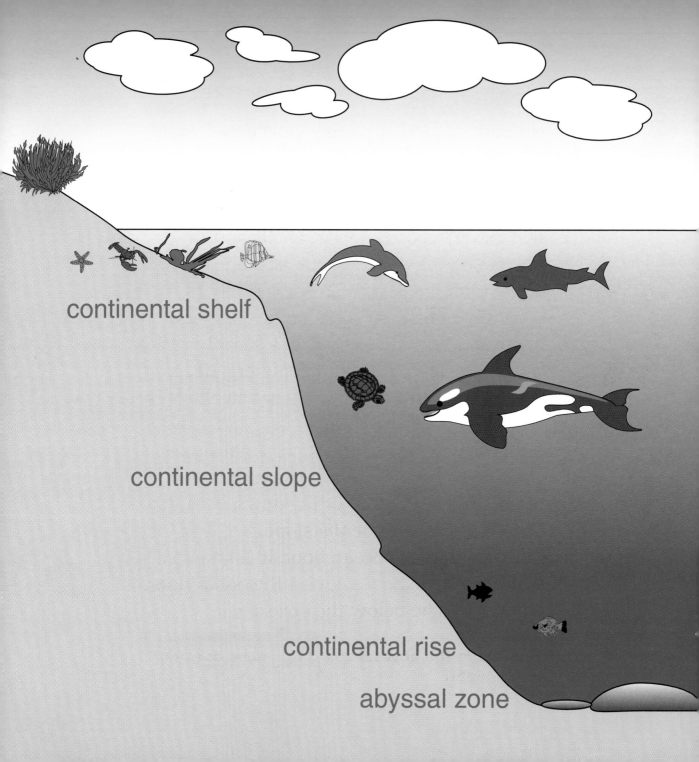

continental shelf

continental slope

continental rise

abyssal zone

The ocean bottom has four zones called shelves. Each shelf lies at a different depth.

The continental shelf is the shallowest zone. It begins at the shore and ends when water is about 600 feet (183 meters) deep. Shells and sand lie on the continental shelf. Sea animals and seaweed live there.

The continental slope starts at the edge of the continental shelf. The slope drops sharply downward. It can be 5 miles (8 kilometers) deep. Many areas of the continental slope have valleys and canyons formed by earthquakes.

Sediment slides down the continental slopes. This mixture of rocks and sand make up the continental rise. This zone also tilts downward. It is not as steep as the continental slope.

The last zone is the ocean floor. It is known as the abyssal zone. Thick ooze covers the ocean floor. Red clay and rocks lie below the ooze.

Few animals live in the abyssal zone. This zone does not receive any sunlight.

Animals in the Ocean

Billions of animals live in the ocean. Many of these animals are fish such as tuna or sharks. Fish breathe oxygen in water through gills. They have strong tails that push them through water. Many fish have sharp teeth used to eat other fish.

Whales and dolphins also live in the ocean. They are mammals. They breathe air through a blowhole. A flap of skin covers the blowhole when they are underwater. Most whales and dolphins eat fish.

Some sea animals cannot be seen without a microscope. They are called zooplankton. Millions of these animals may live in a small area of seawater. Zooplankton look like tiny shrimp.

Many sea animals have ways to protect themselves from predators. The lionfish has poisonous spikes on its body. Clams and oysters hide inside hard shells. Octopuses squirt dark ink at predators.

Spotted flounders hide from their predators in sand. Their scales blend with the sand.

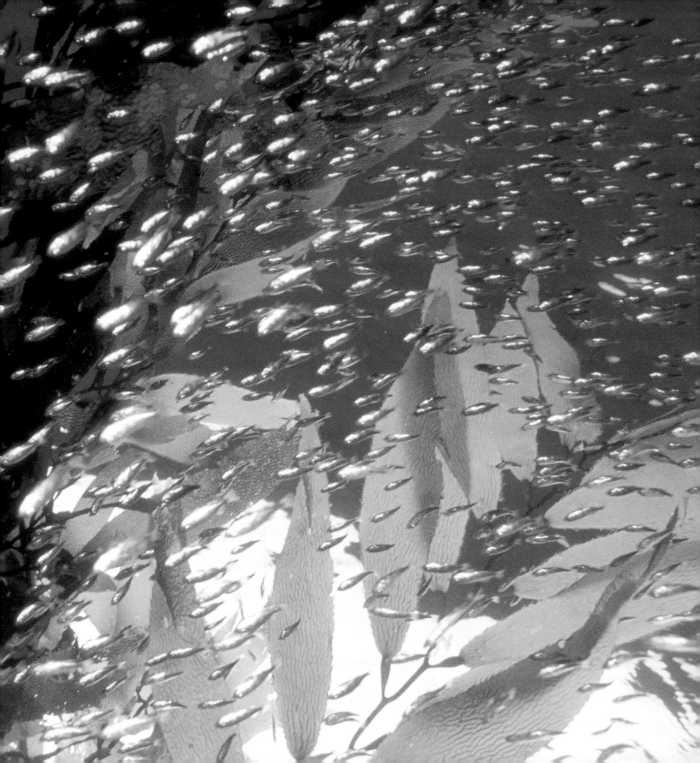

Many kinds of plants grow in the world's oceans. Diatoms are among the smallest plants. They float on the water's surface. Diatoms are so small that people can see them only through a microscope.

Kelp is the biggest plant in the ocean. This giant seaweed grows in cold coastal water. Kelp forests grow in some regions. Kelp can grow as much as 1 foot (30.5 centimeters) a day.

Kelp and other seaweed live on the continental shelf. They grow well in less than 600 feet (183 meters) of water. Kelp and seaweed need sunlight to produce their own food. Sunlight cannot reach deep parts of the ocean.

Seaweed does not have roots and stems for support. Seaweed often grows near rocky shores. The base of the plant holds onto rocks tightly so waves do not wash it away. The leaves sway with the ocean water. Small fish often hide from their enemies in seaweed.

Kelp live on the continental shelf. Many fish swim in this zone of the ocean.

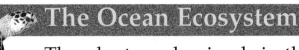

The Ocean Ecosystem

The plants and animals in the ocean are part of an ecosystem. They depend on each other for survival. The climate and water also are part of the ocean ecosystem.

The ocean food chain begins with members of the plankton family. Phytoplankton float in surface waters. These tiny plants make their food from sunlight and water. Zooplankton eat these tiny plants. Animals such as herring and squid then eat the zooplankton. People catch and eat animals such as herring, squid, tuna, and shrimp.

When zooplankton die, they drop to the bottom of the ocean. Animals that live near the ocean floor eat the zooplankton.

Ocean animals are adapted to live at different shelves of the ocean. Animals live only at depths where they can find food. Green sea turtles stay near the ocean's surface. They eat the sea grass that grows there.

California sea lions hunt for squid, herring, and other ocean animals.

The Pacific Ocean is the largest ocean on Earth. It covers 64,186,300 square miles (166,242,517 square kilometers). This area is about one-third of Earth's surface. The Pacific Ocean touches North America, South America, Asia, and Australia.

The Pacific Ocean is the deepest ocean in the world. It has an average depth of 12,925 feet (3,940 meters). The deepest known spot in the Pacific Ocean is the Mariana Trench. This deep ditch is near Guam. The bottom of the trench is 35,840 feet (10,924 meters) underwater. The Mariana Trench is deeper than Mount Everest is high. Mount Everest is the world's tallest mountain.

The Pacific Ocean has 17 other known trenches. These trenches range from 19,700 to 32,800 feet (6,000 to 10,000 meters) deep. Explorers have traveled to these trenches in submersibles. They use special equipment in these underwater vehicles to study the trenches.

The Pacific Ocean borders the western coast of North America and South America.

Fish are one of the ocean's largest resources. People catch about 100 million tons (91 million metric tons) of fish each year. People eat most of the fish. They also make them into vitamins.

The ocean also is an energy resource. Nearly one-third of the world's oil comes from under the ocean floor. People make gasoline, plastic, rubber, and detergents from the oil. Natural gas also lies under the ocean floor.

Workers mine metal deposits such as iron, nickel, and tin from the ocean floor. They make tools and construct buildings from these metals.

Metal and diamonds from the ocean are used to make machines. Saws and drills may have metal blades and bits with diamond tips.

People make jewelry from materials found in the ocean. They create necklaces and bracelets from shells and coral. They also use the ocean's gold and diamonds for rings and earrings.

Commercial fishers catch about 100 million tons (91 million metric tons) of fish each year.

Polluted Oceans

Pollution and waste damage oceans. Ships sometimes spill oil that ruins beaches and kills animals. Birds covered in oil cannot fly.

Litter also threatens the ocean ecosystem. People sometimes leave their garbage on the beach. It then gets swept into the ocean. People also may throw garbage into the ocean from a boat or a ship. Animals sometimes swallow or get caught in people's garbage.

Fishing can threaten the ocean ecosystem. People sometimes catch too many fish. Fish species may become extinct and interrupt the ocean's food chain. People sometimes leave nets in the water. Ocean animals get caught in the nets and die.

Some groups organize ocean cleanups. People gather to pick up trash along beaches. In some parts of the world, divers remove garbage from the ocean floor.

Oil tanker spills destroy the ocean ecosystem.

Hands On: Making Waves

Ocean waves crashing on shore look like they are moving forward. But they are really moving up and down. You can learn how waves move.

What You Need

A piece of rope 10 feet (3 meters) long
A door with a knob

What You Do

1. Tie one end of the rope to the doorknob.
2. Hold the other end of the rope 6 to 8 feet (1.8 to 2.4 meters) away from the door.
3. Shake the rope up and down.

A wave in the ocean moves up and down like the rope.

Words to Know

canyon (KAN-yuhn)—a deep, narrow area with steep sides

current (KUR-uhnt)—the movement of water in the ocean

ecosystem (EE-koh-siss-tuhm)—a community of plants and animals interacting with their environment

extinct (ek-STINGKT)—no longer living anywhere in the world

gill (GIL)—an organ on a fish's side used for breathing

mammal (MAM-uhl)—a warm-blooded animal with a backbone

ooze (OOZ)—very soft mud

predator (PRED-uh-tur)—an animal that hunts other animals for food

sediment (SED-uh-muhnt)—rocks, sand, or dirt

trench (TRENCH)—a long, narrow ditch

Read More

Frahm, Randy. *Ocean.* Mankato, Minn.: Creative Education, 1997.

Lambert, David. *The Kingfisher Young People's Book of the Oceans.* New York: Kingfisher, 1997.

Parker, Jane. *Oceans.* Saving Our World. Brookfield, Conn.: Copper Beech Books, 1999.

Useful Addresses

**Center for Marine
  Conservation**
1725 DeSales Street NW
Washington, DC 20036

Oceanic Society
Fort Mason Center
Building E
San Francisco, CA 94123

Internet Sites

Neptune's Web
http://pao.cnmoc.navy.mil/educate/neptune/neptune.htm
NOAA International Year of the Ocean—Kids' Corner
http://www.yoto98.noaa.gov/kids.htm
OceanLink
http://oceanlink.island.net

Index